Bring Back the Frogs!

Written by Kerrie Shanahan

Illustrated by Meredith Thomas

Flying Start
to Literacy®

Contents

Chapter 1

Back at the farm

"Hey, Jordan, want to go fishing?" asked my cousin Seb.

"Sure!" I said.

Seb is my favourite cousin. He's my age and loves the outdoors, just like I do. We grabbed our fishing gear and set off across the field for our favourite fishing spot. The sun was just beginning to set and it was the best time of day to go fishing.

"You're so lucky to have a stream running through your farm," I said.

Most summer holidays, I stay with Seb and his two brothers on their farm. We go fishing, explore the stream, look for tadpoles and turtles, and stare at the stars at night.

I love the farm!

Don't get me wrong. I love living in the city with my mum, too, but everything is so simple on the farm.

Although, I was about to find out that life on a farm isn't always so simple . . .

It was dusk by the time we arrived at the stream and set up our rods. I loved being there near dusk. The hot sun was almost gone, and the air was cool and still. The stream was our special place, and it never changed.

As I sat waiting for a fish to take my bait, I noticed something . . . it was quiet. Really quiet.

"Hey, Seb?" I said. "I can't hear any frogs."

"Hmmm?" He frowned.

"We can always hear frogs at this time of day," I said. "But this evening, there's none!"

"I hadn't noticed," said Seb. "But now that I think about it, I haven't seen or heard many frogs at all this year."

I loved the sound of frogs – the deep, slow croaks and the high-pitched peeps. It felt strange without them.

What has happened to them? I wondered.

Chapter 2

A suspicious discovery

The next day, my cousins and I went down to the stream. It was a hot day, so before long we were splashing in the clear, cold water.

Afterwards, we dried off in the sun.
But I didn't stay still for long.
I wanted to explore.

"Who wants to go for a walk?" I asked.

"Me," said Seb.

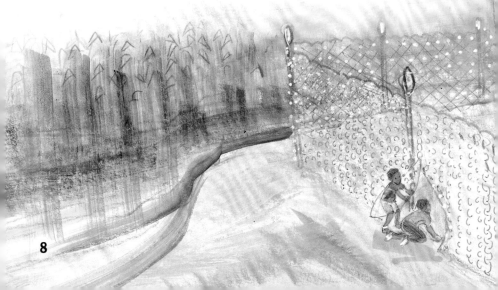

Seb and I followed the stream to the farm's boundary fence. As we went around a bend, I noticed a brand-new, very large warehouse.

"What's that?" I asked.

"It's the new corn factory where Mum works," said Seb.

"Let's check it out," I said.

We stepped through a gap in the wire fence and walked to the back of the factory. Lined up against the wall was a row of large barrels.

"Look at the warning signs," I said. "Those barrels must be full of chemicals."

As we wandered closer, a loud voice startled us.

"What are you kids doing?" the voice called.

Seb and I swung around and saw a person standing at the edge of the stream. She started walking towards us.

"Quick, run!" hissed Seb.

We climbed back through the wire fence and down the bank, and then dashed along the stream.

Once we knew we were safe, we slowed down.

"That person from the factory didn't want us to see those barrels," I said.

"You think so?" said Seb.

"For sure," I said. "And I wonder why?"

Chapter 3

Jordan's dilemma

That night, back at the farmhouse, I couldn't stop thinking about the chemicals we saw at the factory.

"Seb, maybe the factory is polluting the stream, and that's why there are no frogs."

"What do you mean?" asked Seb.

"At school, I learnt that frogs are one of the first animals to be affected by pollution."

Seb looked at me, and I was surprised to see that he was angry.

"Don't go talking about the factory polluting the water," Seb said firmly.

"Why?" I asked.

"If the factory is polluting the water," said Seb, "it might have to shut down. And Mum would lose her job."

"But maybe it's the factory's fault that the frogs have disappeared."

Now, I was angry.

"They're just stupid frogs!" said Seb. "Mum needs that job! Our farm can't make money because of the drought."

"But this can't happen to the frogs," I said. "I'll have to tell someone!"

"Why do you always have to be a hero? Don't say anything to anybody!"

Seb stormed out of the farmhouse.

The next day, Seb was still angry. We had never had an argument before, and it felt strange. I decided to go for a walk to figure out what I should do.

The more I thought about it, the more I was sure it was the factory polluting the water. And that's why the frogs were gone.

Soon, it would affect other animals, too. And if the stream got too polluted, we wouldn't be able to go fishing or swimming.

Should I tell someone? I wasn't sure.
I didn't want Aunt Cath to lose her job.
And Seb had been so upset.

In the end, I decided not to tell anyone about
the frogs, or the pollution, or the factory.

After making my decision, I felt much better.
I headed back to the farm to tell Seb.

Chapter 4

Investigations begin

As I walked back to the farmhouse, I noticed someone standing in the stream. It was the woman from the factory. She was filling small plastic containers with stream water. I watched as she carefully placed the water samples in a bag.

Suddenly, the woman looked up. I tried to hide, but I was too slow.

"Hello there," she said.

She sounded friendly, which surprised me, so I asked her what she was doing.

"I'm testing the water," she told me. "I'm a scientist. Some people around here have been worried that there might be chemicals in the stream."

"Well, I visit every summer and I've noticed there are no frogs this year," I said without thinking.

And then I told her I thought the new factory was polluting the water.

"Thanks for your idea," she said. "I was collecting water samples near the factory yesterday, so don't worry – I'll look into it thoroughly."

As I continued walking back to the farmhouse, I realised what I had done. I had betrayed Seb!

Why did I say that? What will happen when the scientist finds out the pollution is coming from the factory? Will it get closed down? Will Aunt Cath lose her job? Will Seb be mad at me forever?

At dinner that night, Uncle Bernie was talking about the drought.

"The ground is so dry," he said grimly. "And the crops are in bad shape. When we irrigate the crops, the water runs straight off. The ground is too dry for the water to soak in."

"Don't worry," said Aunt Cath in a cheery voice. "I have my job now! And once the rains come, the farm will be fine again."

Suddenly, I wasn't very hungry.

Chapter 5

Answers

A few days later, we were helping Uncle Bernie with the horses when a car drove up the drive. The door opened and a person stepped out. It was the scientist!

My heart started beating at double speed. Did she find out about the factory? What have I done?

My uncle and the scientist shook hands.

"How can I help you, Natalie?" asked Uncle Bernie.

"We have a problem with the stream,"
said Natalie. "When your visitor here told
me that the frogs had disappeared, I knew
we had a real problem."

Everyone turned and looked at me. I could
feel Seb's glare.

"I did some tests," said Natalie. "And there
are chemicals in the stream."

"So the factory *is* polluting the water,"
I said quietly.

"No! Not at all," said the scientist.
"In fact, the factory is very careful about *not* polluting the stream."

"Oh, good!" I said, feeling relieved.

"Unfortunately," Natalie continued, "the pollution is coming from your farm."

Uncle Bernie looked shocked.

Oh no! I thought. Now I've ruined everything!

"Come inside, Natalie," my uncle said.
"I think we need to talk."

When Uncle Bernie and Natalie finally came back outside, Uncle Bernie was smiling. He waved good-bye to Natalie and slapped me on the back.

"Well done, Jordan," he said.

Now, I was really confused.

"After you told Natalie about the disappearing frogs, she realised it was a warning sign," Uncle Bernie said to me. "She found out the pollution in the stream isn't too bad, but it must be fixed."

"But how is the farm causing the pollution?" I asked.

"Well," explained Uncle Bernie, "when we water our crops, the water isn't soaking in. It sits on top of the dry dirt and flows into the stream. The problem is, the water takes the pesticides we use on the corn with it. It's these chemicals that are polluting the stream."

"So can the problem be fixed, Dad?" asked Seb.

"Yes," said Uncle Bernie. "Natalie has organised a meeting with all the farmers in the area. We will make changes to the way we run our farms. It will take time, but we will fix the problem. And that will keep our stream clean and fresh."

"Can we still go fishing?" Seb asked.

"Yes," said Uncle Bernie. "Natalie said the chemical levels are low, so the stream water can't hurt people."

"Well, then let's go fishing," said Seb.

And he gave me a big smile!

Epilogue

Ten months later

"Jordan!" called my mum. "Uncle Bernie's on the phone for you."

I took Mum's phone. "Hello, Uncle Bernie."

"Jordan, good news!" he said. "Natalie has been monitoring the stream and she's happy to say that the frogs are back!"

"That's great!" I was excited.

"So when you visit in just a few months, you can see and hear for yourself," said Uncle Bernie.

"I can't wait!" I said.

A note from the author

I grew up in the country on a small farm. My brothers and I used to look for frogs and tadpoles in our creek, and on summer evenings we could hear the frogs croaking.

When I was doing research about frogs, I learnt what an important indicator they are of a healthy habitat. This reminded me of the noisy frogs from my childhood summers. And this memory sparked an idea for this story.

Today, many children are committed to caring for the environment. This thought helped me to develop the main character, Jordan. Like many of you, Jordan loves nature and wanted to do the right thing about caring for it.